For Audrey,
with love in Christ,
Barbara

Duet for Wings and Earth

BARBARA COLEBROOK PEACE

Barbara Colebrook Peace

sononis
PRESS WINLAW, BRITISH COLUMBIA

LIBRARY AND ARCHIVES CANADA CATALOGUING IN PUBLICATION

Peace, Barbara Colebrook
Duet for wings and earth / Barbara Colebrook Peace.

Poems.
ISBN 978-1-55039-164-0

1. Jesus Christ—Poetry. I. Title.

PS8581.E2D84 2008 C811'.54 C2008-902719-1

Sono Nis Press most gratefully acknowledges support for our publishing program provided by the Government of Canada through the Book Publishing Industry Development Program (BPIDP) and the Canada Council for the Arts, and by the Province of British Columbia through the British Columbia Arts Council and the Book Publishing Tax Credit, Ministry of Provincial Revenue.

Cover art by Erica Grimm-Vance (www.egrimmvance.com)
Edited by Patricia Young
Copy edited by Dawn Loewen
Cover and interior design by Jim Brennan

Published by
SONO NIS PRESS
Box 160
Winlaw, BC V0G 2J0
1-800-370-5228
1-250-226-0077

books@sononis.com
www.sononis.com

Printed and bound in Canada by Friesens.

The Canada Council for the Arts | Le Conseil des Arts du Canada

from the wings of the earth
we heard songs

—ISAIAH 24:16

CONTENTS

Dreaming Yourself Human

I Am Bethlehem

Because You Are Precious in My Sight

Dreaming Yourself Human

Bethlehem Rain

When you first dreamed humankind
was it a hope so
            small and tender
you couldn't mention it yet
even to the self you would become?

Eons passed.
It was still dark.

You were asking yourself,
How far will I have to go?
How much room do I have to make?

Nothing would do but a new earth.
You removed
the roof of your heart—how it hurt
when you pushed the night sky
further apart—

                        Now there was no roof.

Already you could hear
rain falling on a dirt floor.

Song of God: *The night before you were born*

The night before you were born
I brooded
over the waters of uncreated earth. Everything still belonged
to the world of not yet. Under a starless
sky, your image
drifted like seaweed in the tide, *not yet no not yet* in the
form I was to inherit. I
watched for a time you would call *long*, as the wind blew
white spray
          and the waves murmured *not yet no not*
yet; there doesn't have to be a Jesus,
everything could go on
               just the same—

and then, as the waves surged retreated became
becoming
storm-winged,
cresting on the shore of creation, I spoke: *I am that I am*
and the echo, from a long way off:

               Adam.

What was the deepest blue your eye
could distinguish?
What was the worst pain you would ever know?

I stayed in vigil all night,
my hands shaping the gesture of letting go,
till a child could repeat it
with a stone skipped on water.

How much air
you would take in at a breath,
and how long you could sustain it
occupied me for a time you would call *constant*.

All things were before me:

my own necessary death
determined my design for sunlight.

Song of Joseph: *Learning to read*

My father told me Moses stammered too.
The boys jeered: *J-J-J-Joseph,*
s-s-s-say it aguh-again, J-J-J-Joseph . . .

Every night I prayed: *O God,*
Unloose Thou the knot
on my tongue:

when I woke, the serpent was still there.

My father taught me to read and write.
When I looked down at the wax and saw
each word secure
in neat rows, up and down,
like furrows of a field plowed by oxen, I copied
Speak tenderly to Jerusalem,
with my tongue curled against the roof of my mouth,
and the green snake was silent.

At school I read of strange lands and creatures:
Once in three years came the navy of Tharshish,
bringing gold, and silver, ivory, and apes, and peacocks.

What were apes, what were peacocks?

When I climbed the hills in early morning
and watched farmers trudging to the fields,
I could see for miles beyond Nazareth.
From my reading, I knew the land of Iudumaea,
an habitation of dragons, and a court for owls;
I knew the wonders of Solomon's palace,
and the Song of Solomon, where a door opened
into *Behold, thou art fair, my love; behold,*
thou art fair.

Alone in my father's workshop,
I practised speaking my name with Mary's
under the sheltering wings of handsaw and hammer,
rasping wood file;
always I saw their written shapes:
dovetailed, tongue in groove.

I read the scrolls and copied them, learned them
by heart: *Day unto day uttereth*
speech, and night
unto night sheweth knowledge. Gripping
a plank firmly in my hands, I sounded
each word aloud to the stam-
mering angels.

Song of Mary: *At the festival of Sukkoth*

will you take this hut, this temporary shelter
you and I have built together
leisurely of palm and willow, of mud and salt water,
the light a flower opening and closing

will you take this hut,
where the sound of sunlight homing through darkness
sundials my hours with morning and noon

will you take this hut, of three walls only
built of mouse bones and slapped mud
where root and leaf and branch
throw loop and double loop, will you

take this hut, this temporary shelter
and trace on it the deep slope and whorls, the finger
patterns of heaven
                                        will you take this hut, and breathe
into it the fragrance of cedar

will you take this hut, and engrave it with the dusk,
till dark falls unnoticed
in the hollow curves between my bones

This Is the Moment Where in Forever

This is the moment before
God sends the angel to Mary, this

is the moment where in forever
God is leaving home,

walking out alone
into the wilderness.

Out in the wilderness, beyond
the last gate, God has

arrived now at bare rock.
What can he do, but

hold the light in cupped
hands, and offer it to

himself, this
light that keeps on

breaking
and re-forming,

fragile and forsaken,
from the darkness round

a nameless
unmanned
cross?

Song of Mary: *How could I know?*

The first time in my life I saw snow
I was a child, running home through the field.
How could I know what I'd seen?
How could I say what it was?

I was a child, running home through the field.
The flakes landed on my tongue.
How could I say what it was?
The day the angel came and I said *Yes,*

I tasted a new song on my tongue;
I wanted to run and dance and shout!
The day the angel came and I said *Yes*—
How could I know what it was?

To run and dance and shout—*was* that what I wanted?
The apricot sky filled with wings.
How could I know what *Yes* would mean?
From the roof I watched houses move into dark;

the apricot sky was full of wings.
A goat bleated, and fell silent.
I watched from the roof. Houses moved into dark,
the ram's horn sounded for Sabbath.

A goat bleated, and was silent.
I looked at the darkening hills and sky.
The ram's horn sounded for Sabbath.
I thought of the thousands of children not yet born—

I looked at the darkening hills and sky.
How could I know what I'd seen?
I thought of the thousands of children not yet born
and the first time in my life I saw snow.

Dreaming Yourself Human

When my bones were being formed,
carefully put together in my mother's womb,
when I was growing there in secret,
you saw me before I was born.

—PSALM 139:16, 17

Mysterious enough, to wonder about myself in my mother's womb.
But even more strange
to imagine you, dreaming yourself human,
in this, your tiny universe
where no wind blew around the swirling stars,
no thunder stormed.
Yet the same licence to mourn
was written in small print in the marrow of your bone
as there was in mine
when my bones were being formed.

Were you numb then to the touch of stars?
Or did you feel
the breathing of the universe and interstellar space
as there formed in you
the same startle reflex I have when alarmed?
But as you grew there, woven on a loom
with a silk thread boundary
between your mother's dreams and your own,
so I too once grew, dreaming myself human,
carefully put together in my mother's womb.

What were your first dreams, as images swam
naked
through a universe of formless shalom?
Did you hear in Mary's voice, singing
as she scrubbed a bowl clean,
the harmony of the spheres, interpreted in platelet?
As I was patterned on you, so you
patterned yourself to correspond to me,
complex and delicate
when I was growing there in secret.

And you, who graced me
with skin and crowning hair,
shaved your head bare,
a Samson choosing to be his own Delilah;
a lamb and shearer both in one.
For you had risen early, at the break of dawn,
and before any other guests were abroad
you dressed yourself for my birthday,
and wearing the same honourable form
you saw me before I was born.

I Am Bethlehem

Song of Bethlehem

I am Bethlehem. I am not
where you think I am, a circle

on a map. My borders extend
to Afghanistan and Ecuador

I am the valley of the shadow of death

I am the room where you warm your hands
while you're waiting to hear if you have cancer

I am the place where you visit your children
for weekends, when your marriage is broken

I am the prayer you didn't know you were saying.

When you drift into sleep, and somewhere deep within you
it is snowing, I am

Bethlehem: the place where God
tore himself from himself

Song of Joseph: *Journey's Eve*

Frost on the workshop roof.
When I open the door, the comforting

smell of oil mixed with sawdust, and the tools,
each in their own place,

where my candle throws curved, elongated
shadows—

alien to their workaday selves. Once, we were
aliens in this country, and only the tools

gave us connection and belonging, a place
called "Isn't this the son of the carpenter?"

a plow, a yoke, a table, and a roof,
a place we made for ourselves with our own two hands.

Everything is ready, the saddlebags packed
and Mary sleeping . . .

Isn't this the son of the carpenter

I don't
want to go to Bethlehem. I want

to stay here in this workshop, with
the unfinished yoke
and that table I promised my neighbour.

If only the shadows of the tools
could bring my father back,

when I came home from school,
a plow taking shape under his hands,

my father looking up—
Joseph, how did it go today?

and when I ran
          toward him, his enormous shadow—

                    moving to hold my shadow in his arms.

Song of Joseph: *The tally stick*

So many things you taught me, father:
Measure everything twice before you start.

Here's the tally stick
you used to measure me: the rough
notches in the wood, where
a breadth of your thumb,
and the thickness of your palm, shows
even to this day
how I grew from year to year:
          one whole handspan
in that year between eleven and twelve.

But how can I measure
this son who will be mine and yet not mine?

Song of the Donkey

Lord God, there is much I don't understand, and to me almost everything is a mystery.

If I could count the stars and give them names, I could tell you why you named me *Sorrow;* and why my old master beat me every day, so I am marked with stripes along my head and underneath my belly.

Yet, Lord God, you chose me, least of donkeys. You came to the field where I was hobbled for the night; you patted me, fondling my ears; you spoke into my healing welts and bruises and told me that the song of the angels, shepherds, and wise men would be incomplete without me!

Now you send me on a journey with my new master, and a woman who is going to have a baby. The woman strokes my muzzle; she makes for me a bridle of tenderness. Each evening the man brings me fresh hay and water; with gentle words, he makes for me a harness of mercy. My ears swivel to the sound of their voices.

Under the majesty of the stars, I trundle along with saddle sores: this is the only prayer I know.

If you had asked me to carry the sun and moon and stars on my back, I would have knelt and tried. But you have only asked me to join my harsh *heehaw* to the song of the angels. I will sing to you as long as I live. I will open my mouth and bray for the homeless, the lost ones.

Lord God, I have tried to bray your new name and failed; but when all creation catches its breath in pain, I cry out *Heehaw,* and it is the cry of a beaten child, the wheeze of a refugee—

Lord God, I am practising, I am practising all along the road to Bethlehem:

Heeeee . . .
        haw

         H' Jeee . . .
                 haw . . . h's

                 Jh'eee . . . h's saw hs

Is it enough?

Lord God, I can almost say

J'eeee . . .
s'aws.

Song of the Inn

I'm sorry. We don't accept any Samaritans, cripples, or prostitutes,
or any scum like that.
Our apologies for any inconvenience.
It's just that we simply don't have room

for any scum like that.
We can't accommodate any persons who smell of fish or sheep.
It's just that we simply don't have room
for anyone who might disturb our regular guests.

We can't accommodate any winebibbers or drunks
or any persons with blindness, of whatever gender,
who might disturb our regular guests.
It's management policy, nothing personal.

Any persons with lameness, of whatever gender,
and anyone who's illiterate or poor is—
Out. It's management policy, nothing personal.
Our regular guests include top people: scribes and Pharisees.

Anyone blind, lame, deaf, dumb, illiterate, poor, unclean, or
    smelling of donkey—
I'm sorry. You'll have to find a room somewhere else.
Our regular guests include top people: centurions, senators.
We're fully booked at the present time with the Romans taking
    census.

I'm sorry. No room at the present time.
One of our guests is hairdresser to Pontius Pilate.
Fully booked at the present time. (The Romans are taking census.)
Unfortunately, we can't accept any persons with wood shavings
behind the ear.

One of our guests is hairdresser to Pontius Pilate.
Our apologies for any inconvenience.
Unfortunately, we can't accept any persons with wood shavings
behind the ear.
I'm sorry: we don't accept any Samaritans, . . .

Song of the Sheep

This is the holy gospel according to the sheep of Bethlehem, passed down in oral form from age to age.

I want it to be spoken in this holy place, on behalf of all the sheep throughout the world, and translated into language you can understand.

Here it is in Human, coarsely translated from the original wool:

> *Long, long ago there was a stable*
> *where the God of all creatures was born,*
> *and the news came first to sheep and their shepherds,*
> *and there was a lamb*
>
> *who knelt before the human, folding*
> *her knees in innocence. And the news came*
> *first to sheep and their shepherds.*

This is the holy gospel according to the sheep of Bethlehem.

It is a strange bleating, difficult to understand.

Are we more important than we ever dreamed?

But the gospel according to Bethlehem sheep becomes harder yet:

Long, long ago when God was born in human form,
God also became a lamb,
a lamb who was sacrificed for the sin of the world.

This is the holy gospel according to the sheep of Bethlehem.

It is a strange bleating, difficult to understand.

My name is Dolly, and I am a cloned sheep.

I also have wished to journey to Bethlehem.

Song of God: *When I first celebrated Christmas*

I looked back to the time before time was,
remembering how I'd taken seeds of light
and scattered them throughout the dark abyss. Bright
they were for a moment, and then lost
as though they'd turned to dust;
yet from one seed of light
                    arose the star of Bethlehem.

When I first celebrated Christmas,
I looked down on the earth as it was then.
I saw the lights of humans scattered now—
hearth-fire and lamp and candle glow,
and where a stable lantern swung,
the child who was myself, lying among shadows.

The swelling of his lungs in his first cry
stirred grains of hay,
for I was born to share
the air breathed out by cattle and all creatures,
and the atoms of a long since perished star.

My pulse beat in his wrist.
His breath, that stirred
particles of straw,
passed lightly also over moon-dust
as he held Mary's finger in his fist
and slept through his first night:
while galaxies wheeled and passed away.

Because You Are Precious in My Sight

Song of the Moon

In my beginning, when I was nought,
you called my name
as if I were already there
Let there be Moon!

And I was . . . Moon?

Moon.

I have counted the years as I spin around the earth around the sun
as a tree also counts its life in circles, laying down the rings.
And the years have been long enough only to begin
the study of my craft, the art you gave me at birth:
how to bless the earth with moonlight

Now, on this night of your birth,
we meet for the first time face to face, Moon and human,
and I (entering above the half-door of the stable,
praising the hollow of Mary's arm, the pool of shadows
round the manger, and touching
lightly your head)
now render back to you, as you begin from nought,
and lay down at your feet
your gift to me of moonlight.

Song of God: *Because you are precious in my sight*

Because you are precious in my sight,
I make the journey to Bethlehem again and again.
It is much further for me than it is for you.
Each time I make myself
nothing, empty myself of
power and glory. My throat
is hot and dusty from the road.

Because you are honoured,
I have moved over you as light
moves over earth, overshadowing
hills and valleys, oceans and dry land.
I have seeded myself in your womb; I have shaped
your substance in a spiral
and braided it in my eternal name.

Because I love you,
I knock on the door of your silence, listen
for your smallest breath. When you wake
in the night and remember
your nearest loss and furthest longing, I speak
in the rain-washed
hush of your heart; I pour myself
out for you as water.

Because you are precious in my sight,
and honoured, and I love you,
I dream a freedom for you:
I give you at birth and each day
the chance to walk away from me.
But when you cry out to me
from the uttermost parts of your mourning,
I hear you before the words are spoken.
I listen when one atom
in your little finger moves toward me, and I am always
already walking toward you
          on the road to Bethlehem.

Song of Mary: *If I speak with the tongues of rain*

When I rub my hand in gentle circles
over your back to make you bring up wind,
I think of the wind
moving over the face of water
at the beginning of the world,
and it was wind and breath and spirit
all in one word.

When I release you from the swaddling bands,
you stretch and wave your hands in the air,
and gurgle like the rain. When you pucker your lips
and make high piping sounds, I pucker
my lips and make high piping sounds too.
You click your tongue
and when I try to do the same,
you laugh back at me,
and speak in the tongues of rain:
puh puh puh

The rain has such
assurance, there's nothing it does not touch.
If I speak with the tongues of rain,
I say: *hoshta, hoshta*
you say: *nephlee nephlee*
meaning
Let all flesh be gentle.

I teach you all the words I know;
I teach you *breath, wing, feather;* I teach you
abba, daddy, so when Joseph comes home you'll
surprise him, but then I remember—

this is the beginning of your life as a man:
when you shape your mouth and coo,
I know the soft "oo" sounds
prepare you for *bloom* and *moonlight,*
and *Jerusalem.*

It's long past time for your afternoon nap.
My little wildflower, your
petals, still clinging to my shoulder, curl and droop.

Song of the Magi

When we set out, we didn't know how far
or how long we'd be away from home.
It was not the gifts we bore

(gold and frankincense and myrrh)
that mattered on the journey, nor
our quarrels and adventures on the way. It was

learning to look for the star,
and to recognize the star when it appeared.
Sometimes it was clear,

high and brilliant in the sky, outshining
all other stars.
But other times we searched

the four quadrants of the sky and could
see only its absence. Then someone would
point doubtfully—

Well, is that the star?
          You couldn't call that a star
               Anyone can see
it isn't . . .
               the star

We gathered round, uncertain
then set off again, following.

Once when we came
to a mountain stream and saw
the star reflected in a pool,

we knew: the radiant presence
was beneath us also, gleaming
in the mud and rock of earth.

And once when we were passing through
a village too small
to have a name, I stopped

for a child. He was afraid
of the camels. I made mine
kneel;   I picked the child up

from the dust and held him; opened
my saddlebag and offered him
fig cake. He didn't know what

it was. That night when we huddled
round our fire, I thought of
the child

and the way he'd licked the crumbs
from his fingers. I unstoppered a flask, tasted
salt mingled with the wine.

By this time my companions and I
knew each other so well,
we could tell who was speaking

in the dark. We talked about
small things: water and saddlebags,
the best way to tether a camel. We dipped

our bread together in a hot spiced sauce.
We felt young again. Our voices
lifted in song . . .

                              How long since
we'd become so wise, we'd forgotten
a human can be

star-shaped:
two hands, two feet, and a mouth
reaching out to each other

for bread, for comfort, and a journey?

Song of Mary: *You ask me how you got your name*

Sometimes I'd pause
in the middle of kneading bread,
my fingers sticky with flour, thinking
I heard it, or as I climbed the ladder to the roof,
there would be a stirring—

gone before I could see the wings.

In the end it was my sleeping ear
that caught it. Quietly as dew
falls in the night:

Yeshua, Yeshua;

do you hear how it was
you? Listen now when I say it slowly:

Ye . . . sh . . . ua

do you hear the hush
in the middle of your name?
In that hush, Yeshua, I prepared a place

for all the parts of you at home in sunlight
and all the parts of you that lie still in darkness.

"Why," you ask me, "why did God
make a hush
in the middle of my name?"

Perhaps it was because
he wanted to put a bench there
for anyone to sit on,

unspeaking and watching
the water or the stars
or the bright

blue and orange and gold
aurora of our longing.

Song of God: *For Judas not yet born*

to bring up the horizon in relief as clay under a seal,
until all things stand out like the folds of a cloak,
when the light of the Dog-star is dimmed
and the stars of the Navigator's Line go out one by one
—JOB 38:14, 15

Judas, sprawled on the grass, the sun in your eyes as you look up
and laugh, plucking a stalk and whistling between your green-stained
thumbs, saying *This is better than Jerusalem.*
Judas, child of lostness, how could I bear it
if you were not born?
Your features known to me in every detail.
How could I not bring you to birth, when even now
clouds passing over the earth part to reveal
your face in shadow between fire and starlight; even now the daystar
awaits my signal
to bring up the horizon in relief as clay under a seal,

and the angels, who have thousands of different words for light,
have arranged the light around you.
In our little camp on the mountain slope,
Peter and James and John are still asleep;
only you and I stay awake to see the dawn,
our clothes smelling of lentil stew and woodsmoke.
We have stayed up talking, you and I, all night.
Now we wait for the woods and valleys to slowly emerge,
and the long mountain ridges unfold in their beauty, one by one
picking up the sun's spark,
until all things stand out like the folds of a cloak,

the earth in this moment unique; only you and I share.
We are not ready to come down from the mountain.
The wind is passing over the house where you will be born.
If you are not born I could not bear it.
Before we go down from the mountain, we tell each other
what we dreamed:
you dreamed your mother dying
and you tell me your greatest fear,
being left alone at the time of death, no sound of human voice, only
the wind,
when the light of the Dog-star is dimmed.

It is Sabbath, and the morning of your birth. *Shalom, Judas,*
peace be with you;
the earth rising on the first morning of the earth,
fragile blue jewel, my beloved Judas.
Peter and James and John are still asleep.
It is time to come down from the mountain.
Will you remember this, will it be enough to keep you from
despair, when you greet me with a kiss as the men come
bearing torches,
and the last word I speak to you on earth is
Shalom—
and the stars of the Navigator's Line go out one by one?

Song of Mary: *Light falls in parables*

In this room that smells of garlic from our evening meal,
it seems I've only just
got you off to sleep;
that must be why I'm singing so
softly, even I can't hear the words.
I'm old now and tired;   I can't
always hear what people are
saying, though yesterday when I was lying
half asleep, I heard clear enough
when a neighbour leaned over:

She's gone downhill this last year.

Now is the season to lie gazing at the ceiling,
half in the dark
and half in the slanted light from the oil lamp, till
light falls in parables, and turns my shadow
back into a child.
That shape on the ceiling
could be
someone setting out
on a journey of exile, loss, and wandering:
so far away and long ago, it must be
myself, when I was young

somewhere deep within me it is snowing,
quietly, blue snow shadowed with deep gold.

just to set foot is enough;
no need to go anywhere, but just to stand

gazing far across the snow
at the deep shadowed land.

Snow is the holy ghost descending.

Now as I lie
dying, it's snowing again, as
it did when you were born.

Remember how I planned your birth?
I wanted it to be so
beautiful, clean, and orderly,

in my own home, with fresh linen,
water in bowls.
Instead you chose to be born

far from home, laid in a manger—

It was always like that, and the song
I've been singing all my life
is a song about stretching

to enlarge my idea of you, and even
my idea of me. What
were the words, now, how did it go?

My soul doth

(someone is singing softly, I can
hear some of the words now)

magnify . . .

NOTES

The epigraph at the beginning of the book, "From the wings of the earth we heard songs," is derived, after Rabbi Dr. Meir Levin, from the original Hebrew of Isaiah 24:16. In Alexander Cruden's *A Complete Concordance to the Old and New Testament* (1737), the author comments:

> *By the name* wing, *the Hebrews understand not only the* wings *of birds, but also divers things . . .* Wing *is put for the extremity or utmost part of a country,* Job 38. 13. That it might take hold of the ends of the earth, *in Heb. the* wings *of the earth. So in* Isa. 24. 16. From the uttermost part of the earth have we heard songs: *the Hebrew says,* from *the* wing *of the earth.*

Although English versions generally translate the Hebrew *kanaph* here as "end" or, more often, "ends" of the earth, the imagery of "wings of the earth" is preserved in the Septuagint, *apo tōn pterugōn.*

The poem "Song of Joseph: Learning to read" contains five lines from the Bible. "Speak tenderly to Jerusalem" is quoted from Isaiah 40:2, as translated in the New English Bible (1970). "Once in three years . . ." is from 1 Kings 10:22; "an habitation of dragons . . ." is from Isaiah 34:13; "Behold, thou art fair . . ." is from the Song of Solomon 1:15; and "Day unto day uttereth speech . . ." is from Psalm 19:2. These last four are as translated in the King James Bible (1611).

The four glosa lines for the poem "Dreaming Yourself Human" are quoted from Psalm 139:16, 17, as translated in the Good News Bible: The Bible in Today's English Version (1976).

The lines "Because you are precious in my sight, / and honoured, and I love you" in the poem "Song of God: Because you are precious in my sight" are quoted from Isaiah 43:4, as translated in the New Revised Standard Version of the Bible (1989). A minor spelling change, from "honored" to "honoured," has been made for consistency with the rest of the text.

The four glosa lines for the poem "Song of God: For Judas not yet born" are quoted from Job 38:14, 15, as translated in the New English Bible (1970).

ACKNOWLEDGEMENTS

"Song of Mary: How could I know?" appeared in an earlier version in *Kyrie*, by Barbara Colebrook Peace (Sono Nis Press, 2001).

I am enormously grateful to Jayne Postuk, to whom this book owes its origin. It was Jayne who invited me, in 2001, to write poems for performance at the Christmas concert which she and Signi Murgatroyd co-founded, the "Walk to Bethlehem." This invitation, yearly renewed, created the heart of the book. My thanks to the three "divas," Jayne Postuk, Signi Murgatroyd, and Judy Dowling, for the inspiration of their gorgeous voices; to the lively clergy and community of St. George the Martyr, Cadboro Bay, where these poems were first performed; and to all the musicians and readers who made working on this book one of the greatest joys of my life.

I was blessed to receive the great gift of Patricia Young as poetry editor, and I am grateful for her deeply thoughtful and expert shaping of this collection. Many thanks to Diane Morriss of Sono Nis Press, whose extraordinary care for her writers makes her always a joy to work with; to Jim Brennan, for his outstanding book design; to Dawn Loewen, copy editor, for her scrupulous accuracy and poetic sensitivity; to Audrey McClellan, for her expert final proofreading; and to Erica Grimm-Vance, for permission to reproduce her beautiful "angel" paintings on the cover.

I would not have written this book without the lifelong love and inspiration of my sister and brother, Pamela Gormally and Simon Colebrook. Kelly Parsons and Dorothy Field have been wonderful companions on the journey to our threefold book launch, sharing poetic insights over many a cup of tea. I am very grateful to Brian Bartlett, Susan McCaslin, Hannah Main-van der Kamp, Linda Rogers, Peter Sanger, Barbara Stewart, Judy Trueman, and Marga von Rudloff, for their sensitive reading of my work and generous encouragement.

My deepest gratitude to my husband, Terry Peace, who sheltered each poem from genesis to birth, for his loving support and profound understanding.

PHOTO BY TERRY PEACE

Born in northern England, Barbara Colebrook Peace emigrated to Canada in the 1970s for the adventure and to complete a master's degree in classics. She chose to stay in this country and become a Canadian citizen. Having worked for many years as an art gallery manager, she is now a poet, an editor, and a reviewer. Her poetry has been published in various literary journals and anthologies and in her first full-length book, *Kyrie* (Sono Nis Press, 2001). She also co-edited *P.K. Page: Essays on Her Works* (Guernica, 2001). Barbara Colebrook Peace lives with her husband, Terry Peace, in Victoria, B.C.